VOLCANOES

Written by
Nick Pierce

Illustrated by
Liza Lewis

SCRIBBLERS
a SALARIYA *imprint*

This edition published MMXVIII by Scribblers,
an imprint of The Salariya Book Company Ltd
25 Marlborough Place,
Brighton BN1 1UB
www.salariya.com

© The Salariya Book Company Ltd MMXVIII

PB ISBN-13: 978-1-912006-92-2

3 5 7 9 8 6 4 2

A CIP catalogue record for this book is available
from the British Library.
Printed and bound in China.
Reprinted in MMXIX.

Printed on paper from sustainable sources.

Visit
www.salariya.com
for our online catalogue and
free fun stuff.

Contents

Volcanic areas around
the world are shown
on these two maps.

Introduction

Volcanoes can be active, dormant or extinct. An active volcano is likely to erupt. A dormant volcano may seem to be 'sleeping' but it could erupt again. Extinct volcanoes will never erupt again. Most eruptions are violent explosions that spew out lava, ash and gases. Layers of cooling lava build up and can make a volcano grow higher.

On each spread you will have to look for different objects in the main picture.

Fire Mountains

The word 'volcano' comes from the name of the Roman god of fire, Vulcan. He lived under Mount Etna, a volcano in Italy.

▲Vulcan
In Roman myths, Vulcan used the heat and fire of the volcano to forge weapons and armour for the gods.

▲Can you find two pairs of Vulcan's tongs in this picture?

▶How many hammers can you see in this picture?

▲
Can you find
this shield?

▲Can you find
Vulcan's helmet?

▲How many
swords can you see?

The Earth

The Earth is made up of layers. The top layer, where we live, is called the crust. It can be up to 40 kilometres (25 miles) thick. Below that is the mantle, a very thick layer of rock and molten metals. The Earth's core is in two parts: the outer core is hot, molten metal and the inner core is like a solid ball of metal. It is as hot as the surface of the sun!

Can you find...?

The Earth's crust is made up of huge slabs called 'plates'. As they push together, magma can force its way up in between them. This can make volcanoes grow or cause earthquakes.

▲Sea volcano
There are about 5,000 active volcanoes under the sea. Some, like Hawaii, have erupted enough to burst up through the sea to become islands. Can you see the sea volcanoes in this picture?

▲Volcanic dust
Really big explosions can blast clouds of dust and gases many miles into the air. Volcanic dust can be blown all around the world. Can you see the volcanic dust?

Prehistoric Eruptions

Can you find...?

▲Rocks
How many rocks can you count in the picture?

Huge volcanic eruptions in India, 65 million years ago, probably changed life on Earth completely. Thick clouds of volcanic dust surrounded the planet and blotted out all sunlight. The Earth became dark and cold. Nothing could grow. Without food, the dinosaurs may have starved and died.

▲Diplodocus
These huge plant-eating dinosaurs probably weighed as much as a large truck. Can you see them in this picture?

►Eruptions
Magma, gases, ash, dust and rocks all come from erupting volcanoes. The hot magma that flows out of a volcano is called lava.

Lava flows out of the volcano's central crater and from any cracks in its slopes.

◀Can you find this dinosaur in the picture?

▲Tyrannosaurus rex

T. rex had a huge head and quite a big brain for a dinosaur. The biggest T. rex tooth ever found is 30 cm (11.8 in) long. These dinosaurs were one of the last species to become extinct.

▶Trees

Trees can help to absorb the harmful gases released by erupting volcanoes. How many trees can you see in this picture?

Ancient Eruptions

Can you find...?

▲Statue
Can you find
the statue in this
picture?

Can you see
Vesuvius in this
picture?

◀Vesuvius
In 1631, mudflows and lava from
this volcano killed 3,500 people.
It is still very dangerous.

►Columns
How many columns are on this temple?

▼Market
Pompeii was a busy town. Can you see the market shops where the townsfolk would buy their food?

▲Pliny the Younger
The historian Pliny the Younger saw Vesuvius erupt and destroy the towns of both Pompeii and Herculaneum. In a letter to his friend Tacitus he described the earthquakes, the eruption, the lava flows, the huge ash cloud, and the destruction caused.

In 79 AD Mount Vesuvius in Italy erupted. The people living in nearby Pompeii did not know it was a volcano, as Vesuvius had been dormant for 1,800 years. So much rock and ash fell over Pompeii, that the town and its people were soon burned by it. Details of the disaster were described in a letter, written at the time.

13

Undersea Volcanoes

Can you find...?

Tsunami means 'overflowing wave' in Japanese. A tsunami that was 85 metres (279 feet) high hit Ishigaki, Japan, in 1971.

▲Rocks
Scientists have discovered that seabed rocks are only about 200 million years old. That is young compared to rocks on land. Seabed rocks are formed of material from deep within the Earth, thrown up by volcanic eruptions.

Molten lava is made under the sea. It erupts into gaps where the plates of the Earth's crust move apart. Once cool, it forms part of the plate.

An undersea eruption can cause as much damage as one on land. Out in the middle of the ocean, an eruption can trigger a tsunami. The huge waves of a tsunami can travel at 800 kilometres per hour (500 mph).

▶Eeels
How many eels can you see in this picture?

▲Shark
How many sharks can you see in this picture?

Hydrothermal vents
The few living things in the deepest oceans are found near 'hydrothermal vents'. These vents, or openings, are like geysers under the sea. Warm water, heated by magma below the Earth's crust, flows up into the sea.

▶Angler fish
How many angler fish can you find in this picture?

Can you find...?

▲Lava samples

By collecting red-hot lava samples, a vulcanologist can learn more about volcanoes. The heat is so intense that lava can only be collected from small flows. The samples are then taken to a laboratory to study.

▲Protective clothing

Vulcanologists who study eruptions or active volcanoes have to wear protective clothing to reflect the heat from the lava.

Measuring temperature

A thermocouple, a type of thermometer, is put into the lava to measure its temperature.

Studying Volcanoes

People who study volcanoes are called vulcanologists. They visit dormant volcanoes and active volcanoes to watch new eruptions. Studying volcanoes is often dangerous. Vulcanologists have to face high temperatures, poisonous gases, explosions and flying rocks.

Out of the Ash

▲Trees

Trees absorb harmful gases that escape from volcanic craters.

▲Birds

How many birds can you see in this picture?

A big eruption can destroy everything around it. Lava and hot ash burn the plants and kill animals. However, the land recovers amazingly fast. Volcanic soil is very rich in minerals that help plants to grow well. Where there are many plants, there will also be many animals. For example, the beautiful Hawaiian islands were formed from volcanoes.

Shelter

Insects and other small creatures shelter in lichens.

Moss

Moss starts to grow first. Over time, the soil gets thicker and larger plants grow.

▲Dragonflies

How many dragonflies can you see in this picture?

Lichen

Lichens begin to grow on lava after an eruption.

Timeline

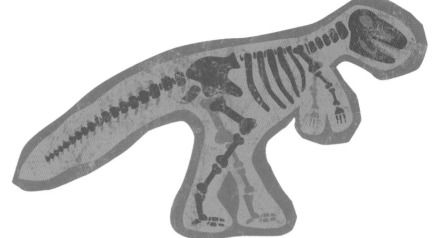

4.5 billion years ago
The Earth is formed.
Early volcanic activity
helps to shape its surface.

65 million years ago
Massive eruptions in India
possibly help cause the
extinction of the dinosaurs.

250 million years ago
Volcanoes in Siberia pump
out billions of tons of carbon
dioxide. This causes global
warming. Most of the planet's
sea life dies. It takes the Earth
5 million years to recover.

55 million years ago
The rock formation called
the 'Giant's Causeway'
in Northern Ireland is
formed from lava.

May 1883
Krakatau in Indonesia erupts, creating the loudest explosion ever heard. Tsunami waves, almost 40 metres (130 feet) high, sweep across neighbouring islands.

1902
The eruption of Mount Pelée on the island of Martinique destroys the city of St. Pierre, killing 29,000 people.

79 AD
The eruption of Mount Vesuvius in Italy destroys the nearby towns of Pompeii and Herculaneum.

1991
The top of Mount Pinatubo is blasted 149 metres (490 feet) into the air. Early warnings of this eruption saved many lives.

Quiz

1. How long ago did the Earth form?

2. What is a volcano called when it is no longer active?

3. What can absorb harmful gases from volcanic eruptions?

4. How many active undersea volcanoes are there?

5. What is the name of the Roman god of fire?

6. What are the three layers of the Earth called?

7. Which two towns were destroyed by the eruption of Vesuvius in 79 AD?

8. Which animals might have been killed off by eruptions in India 65 million years ago?

9. What are people who study volcanoes called?

10. Which volcano erupted in 1883 and produced the loudest explosion ever heard?

Glossary

Active volcano A volcano that shows signs of activity, even if it has not erupted recently.

Ash The powdery material left after a substance has burned up.

Carbon dioxide A common gas produced by all animals in small quantities, and by volcanoes in large quantities. Too much carbon dioxide in the Earth's atmosphere affects the climate.

Core Earth's central layer.

Crust The layer of rock that covers the Earth's surface, both on land and under the sea.

Dormant volcano A volcano that has not erupted for many thousands of years, but could become active at any time.

Lava Molten or liquid rock that flows from volcanoes at very high temperatures.

Magma Molten rock held deep underground in the Earth's mantle.

Mantle The part of Earth that is between the crust and the core.

Pacific Ocean The largest ocean on our planet. It extends from the Arctic Ocean in the north to the Southern Ocean in the south. It lies between the Americas in the east and Asia and Australia in the west.

Plates Individual slabs that make up the Earth's crust.

Tsunami A huge wave caused by massive volcanic eruptions and earthquakes under the sea, far from land. When they reach land, these waves often cause death and destruction.

Index